Library of Congress Cataloging-in-Publication Data

Watts, Barrie.
   Hamster.

   (Stopwatch books)
   Includes index.
   Summary: Photographs, drawings, and text on two
different levels of difficulty follow the stages of
development of the hamster, from mating and birth of a
litter to the time the babies are fully grown.
    I. Hamsters as pets—Juvenile literature. 2. Hamsters
—Juvenile literature. [I. Hamsters] I. Title.
II. Series.
SF459.H3W37 1986   599.32'33   86-10018
ISBN 0-382-09290-2
ISBN 0-382-09281-3 (lib. bdg.)

First published by A & C Black (Publishers) Limited
35 Bedford Row, London WC1R 4JH

© 1986 Barrie Watts

First published in the United States in 1986
by Silver Burdett Company
Morristown, New Jersey

Acknowledgements
The artwork is by Helen Senior.
The publishers would like to thank Jean Imrie and Andrew P. Wright B. Sc. (Hons) for their help and advice.

Hamster

Barrie Watts

Stopwatch books

 Silver Burdett Company • Morristown, New Jersey

Here is a Golden Hamster.

Have you ever kept a pet hamster?
There are lots of different kinds of hamsters.
The one in this picture is called a Golden Hamster.
It is about as long as your hand.

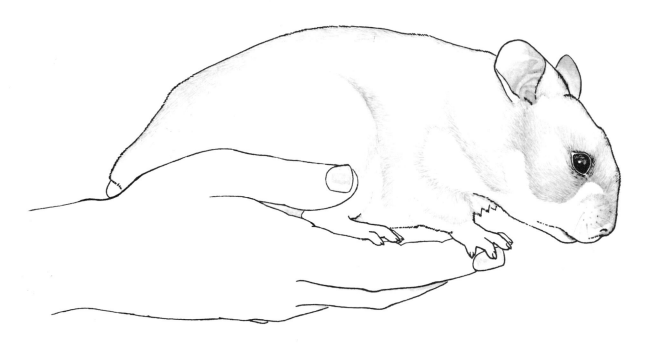

This book will tell you how pet hamsters are born
and how they grow up.

The hamster lives on its own.

Hamsters usually live alone. They only like to be with other hamsters when it is time for them to mate.

This male and this female hamster are mating.

After the hamsters have mated, the female hamster wants to be on her own again. Soon she will have some babies. She will be the mother of the babies and the male hamster will be the father.

The female hamster makes a nest.

Can you see that the female hamster is getting fatter?
The baby hamsters are growing inside her.

Look at the drawing.

The hamster is making a nest for her babies.
She tears up bits of tissue-paper to make the nest
soft and warm.

The baby hamsters are born.

Sixteen days after the hamster has mated, her babies are born. Usually hamsters have seven or eight babies. How many babies can you see in the nest?

The new-born hamsters don't have any hair. Their eyes are closed and covered with skin. Can you see their teeth?

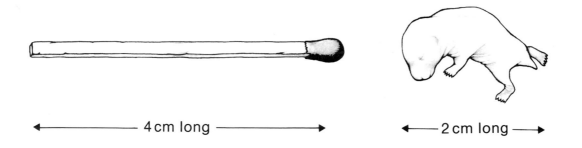

← 4 cm long →   ← 2 cm long →

The baby hamsters are tiny. Here is one next to a match.

The hamsters grow quickly.

Soon the baby hamsters grow soft silky hair.
Look at the big photograph. These hamsters are five
days old. Can you see their tiny ears starting to grow?

These hamsters are nine days old.

Each one is about as long as a match-box.

The mother hamster guards her babies.
She will fight any hamsters who come near the nest.

The hamsters feed on their mother's milk.

Look at the big photograph. The hamsters suck milk from teats underneath their mother's body.

When they are twelve days old, the hamsters start to nibble nuts and seeds. But they still need their mother's milk.

This hamster is fourteen days old.

It has come out of the nest to find food.
Can you see that its eyes are still closed?

The hamsters open their eyes.

The baby hamsters sleep almost all day long.
They snuggle close together to keep warm.

Look at the big photograph. After fifteen days, the
hamsters start to open their eyes. It takes them
a little while to get used to the daylight.
Then they are ready to explore outside the nest.

Sometimes a baby goes too far away. Then the mother
hamster carries it back to the nest.

The hamster makes a store of food.

After four weeks the hamsters stop sucking their mother's milk. They drink water and eat foods like these.

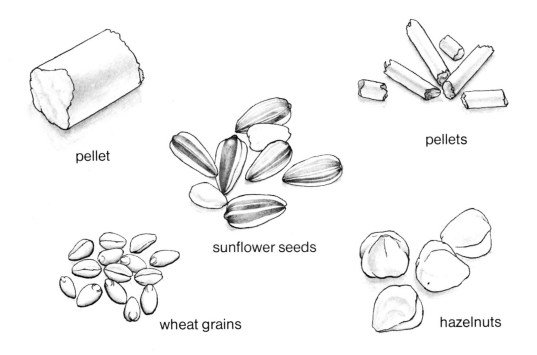

pellet

pellets

sunflower seeds

wheat grains

hazelnuts

The hamsters like to make a store of food.
Look at the big photograph. This hamster is stuffing food into pouches in its cheeks. It will take the food to a safe hiding place.

When the hamster is hungry it will go and find the food.

The hamster cleans its face.

The hamster's teeth are very sharp and they keep growing all the time. The hamster gnaws at nuts and wood. This stops its teeth from growing too long.

Hamsters like to keep clean.
Look at the big photograph. This hamster is using its front paws to clean its face and whiskers.

Now the hamster is five weeks old.

The young hamster is almost as big as its mother.
It likes to climb and explore.

Look at the big picture. The hamster has heard
a strange noise. It stands up on its back legs
and sniffs the air to find out if there is any danger.

Soon the hamster wants to live alone. It starts
to fight with the other hamsters.

The hamster is fully grown.

The hamster sleeps for most of the day.
It curls up in a ball, like this.

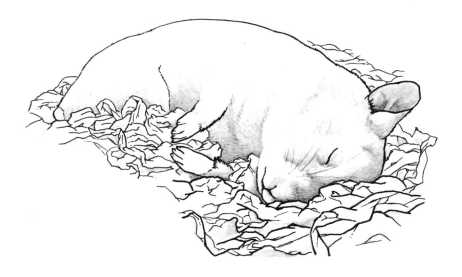

In the evening the hamster gets hungry. It goes to find
its store of food.

After twelve weeks, the hamster is fully grown. Soon it
will want to mate. What do you think will happen if the
hamster finds a mate?

Do you remember how a hamster is born and grows up?
See if you can tell the story in your own words.
You can use these pictures to help you.

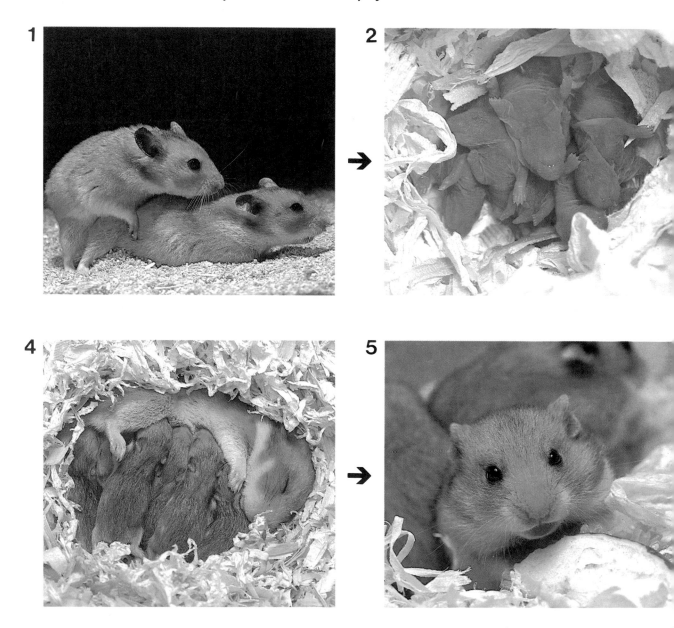

Index

This index will help you to find some of the important words in the book.

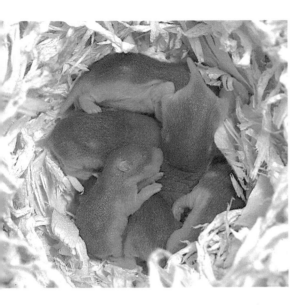

If you keep a hamster as a pet, make sure it has a large cage.
Remember to give it something hard to gnaw and fresh water to drink.
Don't give your hamster too much fruit or greens, it could become ill.